atmosphere press

POEMS

BY

MARTIN

JON

PORTER

NO

HOME

LIKE

A

RAFT

Other poetry books by Martin Jon Porter

Traits

(Ginninderra Press, South Australia,

2016 Picaro Poets chapbook series)

For Sadie Mae

CONTENTS

As he paces in cramped circles, over and over,

the movement of his powerful soft strides

is like a ritual dance around a center

in which a mighty will stands paralysed.

From 'The Panther', by Rainer Maria Rilke

English translation by Stephen Mitchell

'your mind is a prison break free'

etched footpath –
Brunswick, Melbourne

INTERNATIONAL DATE LINE

what happens to time

when you're 1100 metres above Earth

half way across

the Pacific Ocean

about to cross

from daylight to dark

four hours from home

ten hours to unknown

without time

are we without gravity –

a river releasing gold fish

and can it be found

on home ground

when counting shovels

what will happen

if we dare open shutters

that keep routine

will we find

guiding night

in a sea of light?

UPSTREAM

From

base of my

sternum slice

to belly button.

Pry the skin open

with both hands

and peer in.

You'll find a

fish swimming

against the current

with hooks in its mouth.

SCENT

A wolf

crawled

in

to

my lungs.

I inspired its scent and

l o n g e d

to expire its howl.

COMFORT CREATURE

When you skip the full tram...

When you reverse park...

When your day dreams are suppressed...

When you embark
on a new adventure –
the drumming starts again

ONE HORSE TOWN

i'm gonna buy me a horse

to ride away from these limits

i'm gonna buy me a horse

to ride long and hard where air meets air

'We said there warn't no home like a raft...'

from *The Adventures of Huckleberry Finn*

NEW YEAR'S DAY – YUCATÁN PENINSULA, MEXICO

eyes open

a ceiling fan whirs
clicks

its core stable
slowly swaying

as ferries
to and fro docks

as gulls
fly

as waves
softly slap the shore

SUELTA

Seaweed snaps

from stem.

It brushes

with other marine life,

never becoming

tangled

for too long –

guided only by Stars

as the Mayans were.

PORTRAIT OF A PUBLIC BENCH – OLD HAVANA, CUBA

babies:

suckling

their mothers

teens:

listening

to reggaeton

travellers:

tingling

from observations

creatives:

musing

for inspiration

lovers:

dabbing

re-opened wounds

elderly:

reaching

with groceries

dogs:

bones poking through their skin

sheltering

STREETS

The streets

are never narrow

for some –

feeling

finding

new keys scattered on the footpath

every day.

What about those

who walk

the same way

trying to stay

between lines

over sprayed?

BOW

Feet dangling from vestibule steps on the train,

looking back at all the carriages...

smooth footpaths

dogs and cats that are contained

easy access to wi-fi

toilets that flush

endless supply of toilet paper

gutters that drain after a downpour

cars with anti-pollution systems

convenience stores

supermarkets

knowing where to buy tissues and pens

electronic payment machines

public rubbish bins that are collected regularly

drinkable tap water

high pressured hot showers

hassle-free from prostitutes

technologically advanced classrooms

The old man selling flowers at the station before
departure –

his head bowed at one CUC, mine is still bowing

LA MUJER DE ANTIGUA, GUATEMALA

after rising early

and cooking breakfast

for travellers

she washed

their dishes

and sang

'to the ceiling

lungs clinging'

a song

not many westerners

could interpret

UMBILICAL DARKNESS

under moon

in rain

across sky

amidst trees

above water

atop ruins

up mountains

down volcanoes

on rooftop terraces

through languages

among people

out in this

umbilical darkness

there aren't any pangs

of stray dog fights

AUSTRALIAN ASTRONAUT

At 8pm, a bus drops me on the outskirts of Santa Ana –
El Salvador.
No street lights in this galaxy.
The bus attendant also gets off,
his shift finished for the night.
Says there is a bus I can catch with him to Juayúa
in the Ruta de las Flores region.

Local currency is USD, and I have none.
There are two service stations
that orbit a busy intersection.
The first has no ATM.
After leaving, I see the attendant catch his bus.
The second is about to close,
so I run in with my traveller's backpack asking for
"cajero automático".
The shop assistant holds up a car deodoriser.
Eventually, she allows me to withdraw $25.
I fumble in limited Spanish
and learn there are no more buses
heading to Juayúa tonight.

I ask for recommendations of nearby hotels.

There is one, but it's

"muy peligroso caminar solo por la noche".

In the short time there,

I seem to have gathered an audience

smiling and waving goodbye.

Next thing, I'm straddling a motorbike

behind one of the service station attendants.

No helmets.

We swerve turning trucks and buses on a road with an

icy crust.

I'm chauffeured into a garage

and choreographed to press a button,

which closes the electric roller door.

Then I walk upstairs to a room.

There is pay TV with a soccer match,

salsa music,

globular cluster disco ball

and horizontal mirror parallel with double bed.

I try to force the balcony door.

Two men are yelling orders

through a two-way black hole.

I run downstairs,

press the button and walk out into the driveway.

There's a man with a clipboard,

no official attire.

There's a younger man with a bumbag –

his official attire.

They explain their protocol as

"la seguridad, porque es muy peligroso aquí".

I return with the younger man

who provides a menu as reassurance.

He recommends the microwave pizza, cup of noodles

and a can of Coke.

They're delivered through the two-way black hole.

At 7am, I send word for a taxi via gesture satellites.

Within 15 minutes, there's one waiting in the garage

below my room.

Windows tinted beyond any legal limit.

The driver introduces himself –

Oscar.

I point to the address of a bus terminal.

We make it.

Eating breakfast tamales in a patisserie,

the sole customer,

through its speakers 'Don't Change' by INXS

pulls me back…

I'm standing here on the ground

The sky above won't fall down

See no evil in all direction

FORWARD

Momentum

moment *um*

mo – men – tum

momentum

moment *um*

mo-men-tum

momentum

moment *um*

momentum

...

ON THE WOLF TRAIL

I am a wolf
always preferring
to observe.

I keep swift feet,
avoiding body contact
in close.

Loose skin
hanging
around my neck,

never permits
sink-searching
fangs.

Fur between pads
is all that can be traced
before pouncing,

assertive only
to restore
nature's equilibrium.

I feel stronger
roaming alone
than in a pack.

As my kind
find it difficult
to bark,

peripheral
and night vision
detect dogs.

They search
for a master –

I am always
hunting
for a place.

Onto the
wolf trail again.

BLANKETS

why do we cover ourselves
in blankets…

if we're warm
all the time
how can it be known
if we're still warm

and our
bare
skin –

does it
withstand
the elements
without blankets

what happens
when our blankets
develop holes

are they stitched

or shed?

LONELINESS

I
prefer to dress
in black.

I'm
always lurking
even in groups.

I
have a knack
of finding
shadows in your soul,
seeping into them.

I
enjoy seeing
how long you can withstand
my
acid flushing
through your chest.

Sometimes

I

don't speak

any language at all –

a weight vest

that clings.

Only certain types

aren't afraid of

me.

They gain strength from

my

do-gooding,

self-reliant twin –

Solitude.

He saves them

from rising water

when floating neck deep

in a dark tunnel.

CARTAGENA WALLS

my chest
floating again

no longer a vessel
moored by ambition –

beyond old walls
there's always a new city

COLUMBIAN CUPID

listening to midnight

he ducks and slides

through a hostel entrance

in El Poblado, Medellin –

slight sweat beading

pleated slacks and open collar

olive skin

fewer wrinkles than there should

side slicked brown hair

minutes shaved from face

he re-emerges in the lounge area

sporting an ensemble of sandals

silky tracksuit pants

and lemon Penguin polo

a joint passes

between several twenty- and thirty-somethings –

he doesn't decline

through the smoke

sneakily tugging

eye corners

is a glint

BHAGAVAD GITA

i'm hunched over a table

in the corner

of a Krishna restaurant

Palermo, Buenos Aires

drinking tea

and eating curry

to humming speakers

petite furniture

with tasselled paisley coverings

and dim lamps

with sequin shades

wrap

this space

around me

no need

for battlefield discussions

between Arjuna

and his charioteer

INHALE

a book with

sun wrinkles
in its cover

slight tears
from backpack cramming

dog ears
frowned upon in schools

condiment
fingerprints

waltzes
of annotations

patience
on a bed side table

has been inhaled

just like the ones

in Buenos Aires

95

What do you write
to Nan
for her 95th birthday
when she's stopped
eating and drinking…

In Colonia, Uruguay,
but I'll be home soon.
I heard the news
you're still talking and breathing,
that it won't be long
before you'll be leaving.

I'll say goodbye
on my knees,
salt soaking
into your earth.

HOSTELS

CHECK-IN: to sauna dorms
with ceiling fans combusting
fumes of spew and body odour

1AM – snoring Olympics

3AM – pants and long sleeve shirt
allied forces
against invading territorial bed bugs

5AM – heavy breathing and creaky bunking
planting condom land mines

7AM – backpacks zipping
plastic bags rustling
shower water crackling

7.30AM – bathroom floor a wading marsh
begging scientific investigation

9AM – breakfast included

with political rants over joints

CHECK-OUT: a resident cat licking the kitchen tap

SALKANTAY, PERU

i am

ice
water
lake

seed
stem
tree

dust
dirt
clay

but mountains have
epochs of rocks –
travellers can only
carry cairns

'Let your soul be sated

with the odd beauty of this landscape'

from 'Natural Wonder', by Alfonso Ricciutto

HOMECOMING

I'm called "babe"
and "mate"
at the airport.

A father disciplines his child,
"Oi!"

There's an unclaimed coffee order,
"Sharon?"

The taxi driver tells me
about a nearby river
"full 'a' crocs".

No one stares
at my thongs.

I awake
to sun and blue sky
creeping through the curtains.

Cockatoos and magpies
are squawking in the trees.

A stubby of beer
is rattling in the fridge.

There's a message from Mum,
"Would you like a BBQ for tea?"

A dog approaches me
for a pat, not food –
it has a collar
with registration tags.

SALT LICK

This road

it begs me

a dog

who's tasted

fresh meat

can't go back

to kibble

that smell

it begs him

again

and again

HIGHWAY SOUL PATROL

heading north

from blue skies into dark clouds

trying to find the other side

away from where

freedom is sailing in sync

with sequence green lights,

leaves flirting under car tyres

to a place where

mid-river gums

never seem overcome

and worker ants carry

icing to their nest

away from where

cars ram behind trams

searing syllables into backs

stiff with one quarter of a dream

to a place where

I can wipe wide open spaces

into eyes,

release them from squeezing pickets

away from where

people wear wristwatches for time,

always racing the sunset

to a place where

I can let legs

move mind

sweat city smog from pores

and anthologise thoughts

in vacant streets

to that place on patrol

for the pressed flower

in my soul

so it doesn't become carrion

JEWELL STATION, BRUNSWICK

I saw you
on the other side
of the station
today.

You were near
the entry
and I was near
the exit.

You were pacing
and fidgeting.

When the train
had finished
flashing between us,
you were gone.

And then the fish swam away.

ACKNOWLEDGEMENTS

The following poems have been previously published:

'Scent' and 'La Mujer de Antigua' in *Her Heart Poetry*

'Forward' in *Unusual Work*

'Homecoming' in *Idiom 23*

'Portrait of a Public Bench – Old Havana, Cuba' and 'Loneliness' in *ArtAscent*

'Salkantay' and 'Salt Lick' in *Wanderlust Journal*

'On the Wolf Trail' in *Wild* (Ginninderra Press)

'Streets' in *What Rough Beast* (Indolent Books)

ABOUT ATMOSPHERE PRESS

Atmosphere Press is an independent, full-service publisher for books in genres ranging from nonfiction to fiction to poetry, with a special emphasis on being an author-friendly approach to the challenges of getting a book into the world. Learn more about what we do at atmospherepress.com.

We encourage you to check out some of Atmosphere's latest releases, which are available at Amazon.com and via order from your local bookstore:

The George Stories, a novel by Christopher Gould

Mere Being, poetry by Barry D. Amis

The Traveler, a young adult novel by Jennifer Deaver

Mandated Happiness, a novel by Clayton Tucker

The Third Door, a novel by Jim Williams

The Yoga of Strength, a novel by Andrew Marc Rowe

They are Almost Invisible, poetry by Elizabeth Carmer

Let the Little Birds Sing, a novel by Sandra Fox Murphy

Carpenters and Catapults: A Girls Can Do Anything Book, children's fiction by Carmen Petro

Spots Before Stripes, a novel by Jonathan Kumar

Auroras over Acadia, poetry by Paul Liebow

Channel: How to be a Clear Channel for Inspiration by Listening, Enjoying, and Trusting Your Intuition, nonfiction by Jessica Ang

Gone Fishing: A Girls Can Do Anything Book, children's fiction by Carmen Petro

Owlfred the Owl, a picture book by Caleb Foster

Love Your Vibe: Using the Power of Sound to Take Command of Your Life, nonfiction by Matt Omo

Transcendence, poetry and images by Vincent Bahar
     Towliat
*Leaving the Ladder: An Ex-Corporate Girl's Guide from the
     Rat Race to Fulfilment*, nonfiction by Lynda Bayada
Adrift, poems by Kristy Peloquin
*Letting Nicki Go: A Mother's Journey through Her
     Daughter's Cancer*, nonfiction by Bunny Leach
Time Do Not Stop, poems by William Guest
Dear Old Dogs, a novella by Gwen Head
Bello the Cello, a picture book by Dennis Mathew
How Not to Sell: A Sales Survival Guide, nonfiction by
     Rashad Daoudi
Ghost Sentence, poems by Mary Flanagan
That Scarlett Bacon, a picture book by Mark Johnson
Such a Nice Girl, a novel by Carol St. John
Makani and the Tiki Mikis, a picture book by Kosta Gregory
What Outlives Us, poems by Larry Levy
Winter Park, a novel by Graham Guest
That Beautiful Season, a novel by Sandra Fox Murphy
What I Cannot Abandon, poems by William Guest
All the Dead Are Holy, poems by Larry Levy
*Rescripting the Workplace: Producing Miracles with
     Bosses, Coworkers, and Bad Days*, nonfiction by Pam
     Boyd
Surviving Mother, a novella by Gwen Head
Who Are We: Man and Cosmology, poetry by William
     Guest

ABOUT MARTIN JON PORTER

Martin Jon Porter grew up in Ballarat and studied teaching in Adelaide, but now lives in Melbourne with his family. His first collection of poetry, *Traits*, was a chapbook published in 2016. His poems have been published in Canada, USA, UK, Australia and online.